DEDICATION

This manual is dedicated to our Heavenly Father, the Creator of all. It is through His divine vision that RARE-9 was inspired two years ago to use his spiritual gifts, spirituality, giving, helping, leadership, hospitality, and compassion to co-author this mentor/mentee workbook.

This workbook is dedicated to black youth, teenagers, and young black men, with the hope that it helps them to live in peace and harmony with one another.

In closing, we extend heartfelt thanks to the entire Hitch family, whom some have gone to be with the Lord. They were exemplary role models, both men and women, who shaped us into the individuals we are today. Special acknowledgment goes out to Rev. Dr. Luther Mckinney Jr. (Co-Author), whose guidance and support in this endeavor has been invaluable.

Copyright

Table of Contents

RARE-9 JAGUAR MENTORSHIP ORGANIZATION
406 Flume Road
Elgin, South Carolina 29045
Website: rare9jaguar.com

INTRODUCTION TO RARE-9 MENTOR/MENTEE WORKBOOK

The essence of this workbook is to allow black youth/teenagers to feel empowered and free with a sense of freedom to embrace positive self-esteem as they travel through a world of racism, discrimination and bullying. The name RARE-9 is more than a word put together to sound odd or fancy. The first "R" stands for respect. What a different world we all would experience if everyone displayed respect among one another. The Council on Quality and Leadership defined respect as "the means to demonstrate "high regard" for or special attention to something or someone." The Council goes on to say that respect has personal definitions that are influenced by our own personality, emotions, preferences, and cultural context. The second letter "A" highlights admiration. According to Oxford Advanced Learner's Dictionary admiration means in the noun form, a feeling and liking for someone or something, such as to watch or gaze in admiration. However, in the verb form, Oxford stated that admiration means to respect someone for what they are or for what they have done, such as I admire her for sticking to her principles and standards. The second "R" in RARE-9 pertains to rationalization. The Merriam-Webster dictionary stated that rationalization is "a way of describing, interpreting, or explaining something (such as bad behavior) that makes it seem proper, more attractive, etc. "From a RARE-9 perception an individual can either make a rational or irrational decision. Many individuals make irrational decisions by not thinking things through clearly enough causing unnecessary problems or issues at school. The "E" stands for everyone. Simply put, it will take everyone on this planet to show respect among each other if we are to enjoy peace, life, love, serenity, and joy more abundantly. Where does the nine (9) come into view with the RARE-9 theory. During the early 2000 years, it was clearly stated in various meetings, TV news, around radio/internet news that the Pipeline-to-Prison targeted black youth from the third grade until the twelfth grade which is nine (9) years. Secondly, my birthday is September 9. In 1999, I had all 9s on my birthday. The points explained previously describe the true meaning behind RARE-9.

The mission, vision, values, and expected outcomes are self-explanatory, however may change from time to time based on what is happening in society, for example, gun laws are changing periodically for different states and we may have to make amendments to our literature to keep up with the many changes that occur. The Logo is a symbol of discipline, leadership, strength and empowerment. It signifies to black male students to understand that your best potential comes when you give your best and that becoming lackadaisical or lazy is not an option. Last, but not least, the twelve-step program is designed to help empower black male students and provide twelve (12) step nutrients to the soul, body, and mind ultimately yielding a successful journey through their educational life.

RARE-9 Jaguar Mentorship (RJM) Program is written "to keep it simple.". Its theoretical framework derives from the Social Learning Theory. Bandura (1997) emphasizes the importance of observing and modeling the behaviors, attitudes, and emotional reactions of others. Due to peer pressure, it is possible to see an enormous number of changes in behaviors, attitudes, and emotions among black male students. It is important to provide black male students with leadership tools to allow them the opportunity to be leaders and not followers. This RARE-9 Theory will teach black male students the importance of self-leadership, transactional leadership, and transformational leadership.

The RJM framework consists of the first perspective which is the LEAP perspective. Within this perspective the words can always be changed to challenge black males who are within the group. This perspective will also increase their vocabulary and have them able to communicate, rationalize and think on a higher educational level. The LEAP perspective is more about being successful down the road and can be done as a written or mental exercise. RARE perspective or Climbing the Ladder is the second perspective. When a black male student has reached an endless road and feels deflated, this perspective uses a scale from Good to Very Good, with a number scale from 0 thru 10 in determining how well a black student can bounce back after having an uneventful or stressful day. The Climbing the Ladder perspective can also be a written or a mental exercise. The third perspective is the Conversation perspective. This perspective is created to address black male's overall problems. This is strictly a mental exercise and can be utilized as a student or group exercise. The Immediate Conflict Resolution & Tango (Face-to-Face Virtual Process) is the final perspective. This perspective is used by mentors and mentees when the parent or guardian has agreed to the RJM program providing after hour mentor services to their black male student(s).

Finally, there is a book named "Their Name is Today (Reclaiming Childhood in a Hostile World)" written I believe for parents to get a better understanding of parenting and family bonding. In this book, Malcolm X stated how the child is now the leader of the household, is he right or wrong? Also, there is a poem (I Will

Not Die an Unlived Life by Dawna Markova) that black male students can embrace. This poem will have them think about their serenity and a productive future. Please note that the remaining information in this workbook is equally important but written specifically to obtain a greater understanding and the guidance through our program. In the last portion of this workbook we have included an example of a Business Plan for informational purposes only. This may also help young black males who are thinking about starting a business.

Minister RARE-9 & Dr. Luther McKinney Jr. presents

(A program based on over thirty years of observation, clinical, educational & hands-on experience)

RARE-9 MENTOR/MENTEE WORKBOOK:
Includes Mental and Handwritten Exercises

(Single Mothers/Guardians, Mothers, Fathers, DJJ, DSS, Mentor Businesses and school systems should embrace this ideological RARE-9 perspective.)

Authors:

Dr. Luther McKinney Jr., PhD., CCPSS, USMC, Retired

Minister RARE-9, M.Ed., M.A., CAC-AD, USMC, Retired

RARE- 9 JAGUAR MENTORSHIP ORGANIZATION

MISSION

The mission is to mentor third grade through twelfth grade black males in becoming the cornerstone of education, financial success, security, spirituality, and strength in our communities. Also, to provide a safe place for services, mentorship, leadership, advocacy, motivational speakers, tutoring, counseling, and scholarship guidance. This organization will mentor all youth and make appropriate referrals as deemed necessary.

"Special Mission"

Hold mentor/mentee educational sessions, classes, seminars, and presentations on saying "NO" to guns topics. Educational sessions will comprise of the mentees ages five to eight along with parent(s) and guardian(s). The organization will provide aftercare mentorship educational sessions for Department of Juvenile Justice teenagers being released back into society. Provide mentor advocates with a holistic perspective to mentoring, educating, supporting, and networking to bring structure with student mentee, parent/guardian, and all other stakeholders in the success of the mentee's education. Finally, we will make a grave attempt to direct some mentee's career path to joining the United States Marine Corps: The Few, The Proud, The Marines.

RARE-9 JAGUAR MENTORSHIP ORGANIZATION

VISION

The RARE-9 Jaguar Mentorship organization is the Premier Mentor Program for Disabled, At-Risk, Gay, Bi-Sexual, Troubled, 3rd Grade through 12th-grade black male youth. This program is rooted in self-esteem; meaning these youth can survive and thrive in a system that provides nutrients for the soul. RARE-9 Jaguar establishes a book and guide that mentees can use in times of perils. The end result will be that 80% of the mentees will be successful and productive youth graduating from school while retaining the following as future growth tools:

R - RESPECT

A - ADMIRATION

R - RATIONALIZATION

E - EVERYONE (LOVE OTHERS)

9 - THE PIPELINE TO PRISON EQUALS 9 YEARS

The organization will create mentor advocate positions responsible for mentees twenty-four hours a day, five days a week and a team player with all stakeholders. The mentor advocate will be aware of what is going on with the mentee, attending and reporting on all meetings, home visits, when the mentee has counseling sessions, doctor's appointments, school Individual Educational Plans and 504 Behavioral Modification Plans. The organization will hold sessions on saying no to guns for black males from five years old to eight years old. (Parents/guardians must accompany the black male mentee.)
It is possible that Barber Shops will also be established as Mentorship Hubs.

RARE-9 JAGUAR MENTORSHIP ORGANIZATION

VALUES

The values that will contribute to the overall success from this mentor organization includes: Respect, mentee-centeredness, to increase motivation not procrastination, quality over quantity, accountability, professional, self-leadership, teamwork, and integrity. Mentees will understand the concept of "Stop, Think and Act/React" for improved behavior, decision making and impulse control. Finally, the use of non-violence and avoidance of any type of weapon(s).

RARE-9 JAGUAR MENTORSHIP ORGANIZATION

"MOTTO"

NEVER SETTLE FOR LESS WHEN YOU CAN ACHIEVE

THE BEST

RARE-9 JAGUAR MENTORSHIP ORGANIZATION

Outcome Expectations

1. While mentor advocate(s) are visiting the school system (shadowing mentee student) allow them to connect with students in such a manner that student issues are resolved in a timely manner, allowing students to return to the classroom with no more interruptions.

2. Reduce the time that school officials spend with black males responding to student problems and issues.

3. Reduce the number of Individual Education Plans and 504 Modification Behavior Plans among black male mentee students).

4. Introduction of a third party that can bring about mediation in an impartial manner and without prejudice.

5. Effective learning mentor advocate process that teaches the black male students to take responsibility for their action, so that they do not occur over and over again causing unnecessary school disruptions.

6. Over a period of time show less class room referrals, in-school suspensions, detentions, and suspensions.

7. Most importantly, create an atmosphere and bond where students, teachers, parents or guardians and school administrators work together in harmony to accomplish the desired goal of students receiving their education.

8. Introduction of student concepts (from mentee's mentor program) that will reduce student conduct behaviors.

9. The goal of helping students through a supportive and successful mentor advocacy program, rather than a goal to make a monetary profit.

10. Show an improvement in graduation rates on a year-to-year basis, pertaining to black male students.

RARE-9 JAGUAR MENTORSHIP ORGANIZATION

MENTEE TWELVE STEPS FOR A BELOVED COMMUNITY

1. Recognize you have power over what happens in your everyday life. Utilize self-control to stop, think, and react when faced with a problem or crisis.

2. Come to believe that you can achieve anything you put your mind to, while being honest and truthful about your conviction (s). Reach out to your higher power when necessary.

3. Realize you control your own destiny by the decisions you make now.

4. Take responsibility for your own actions while showing maturity to apologize to those you have offended or hurt.

5. Report any situation that hinders or prevents you from having a safe and productive school, home, or any other environment. Situations students may want to report are the following:

   * Sexual assault or any other illegal sexual act
   *gun violations
   * bullying
   *illegal drug incidents
   * social media violations and acts of terrorism

6. Learn to know the people, places, and things that contribute to an excellent self-esteem level and lifestyle.

7. Do not accept failure, but challenge yourself to find a solution for positive outcomes. Please contact a support system, such as, parent/guardian, mentor, mental health therapist, teacher or church leader.

8. Never accept suicide or violent behavior as an alternative to solving a problem

9. Understand the importance of making good and timely decisions.

10. Never accept "NO" as a final answer or decision and talk with your mentor at least three times a month to discuss various situations/need for guidance.

11. Learn to channel negative energies into positive energies and do not convert to a negative leader under any circumstances.

12. Take time out to exercise, to enjoy leisure, take prescribed medication(s), and to reduce stress, while keeping things simple as a productive citizen.

RARE-9 JAGUAR MENTORSHIP PROGRAM

"KEEP IT SIMPLE"

RARE-9 Jaguar Mentorship Program's Theoretical Framework

Social learning theory forms part of the basis of the theoretical framework for the RARE-9 Jaguar Mentorship Program. Bandura (1977) emphasizes the importance of observing and modeling the behaviors, attitudes, and emotional reactions of others. Social learning theory defines human behavior in terms of the continuous reciprocal interaction between cognitive, behavioral, and environmental influences (Bandura, 1977).

The optimal learning environment is one where a dynamic interaction between instructors, learners and tasks provides an opportunity for learners to create their own truth due to the interaction with others (Miller & Dollard, 1941). It has been established that Categories of Knowledge and Reality are actively created by social relationships and interactions. Effective reinforcements directly affect the learned behaviors and their frequency of occurrence. Positive attention given from peer group members or other group members influences the positive degree of learning that occurs and is continued (Bandura & Walters, 1963).

In addition," Transformational" and "Transactional" Leadership establish the remainder of the framework for the RARE-9 Jaguar Mentorship Program. We will first identify the definition of Transformational Leadership and list the characteristics and benefits of this leadership style. Secondly, we will discuss the characteristics and benefits of Transactional leadership. Lastly, we will explain how these three theories work in unison to provide the help needed by the client.

Northouse, P (2000), defines transformational leadership as a process that changes and transforms individuals. Values, ethics, standards, and long-term goals are the major focus of transformational leadership. Transformational leadership focuses on assessing followers' motives, satisfying their needs, and treating them as human beings in the process.

Using very specific attempts to influence followers on a one-to-one level to very broad attempts to influence whole organizations and even entire cultures, transformational leadership is an encompassing approach. Followers and leaders are bound together in the transformational process. Burns, J.M. (1978), links the roles of leadership and followership. Burns states that leaders are those individuals who tap the motives of followers in order to better reach the goals of leaders and followers. Leadership is inseparable from followers' needs.

Bass (1985) broadened the scope of Burn's work by giving more attention to followers' needs rather than leaders' needs. Bass suggested that transformational leadership could apply to situations in which the outcomes were not positive. Bass also suggested that charisma is a necessary but not sufficient condition for transformational leadership and gave more attention to the emotional element and origins of charisma.

Weber (1947) provides the most well-known definition of charisma as a special personality characteristic that gives a person superhuman or exceptional powers, is or divine origin, is reserved for a few, and results in the person being treated as a leader. Weber also recognizes the important role played by followers in validating charisma in these leaders (Bryman, 1992; House, 1976).

House (1976) informs that charismatic leaders act in unique ways that have specific charismatic effects on their followers. Charismatic leaders are dominant, have a strong desire to influence others, are self-confident, and have a strong sense of one's own moral values. Personality characteristics of charismatic leaders include: strong role models for the beliefs and values they want their followers to adopt; appear competent to followers; possess articulate ideological goals; communicate high expectations for followers; exhibit confidence in followers' abilities to complete goals; and arouse task-relevant motives of followers that may include: affiliation, power, or esteem.

House (1976) also identifies several effects that are the direct result of charismatic leadership. These effects include; follower trust in the leader's ideology, unquestioning acceptance of the leader, follower obedience, emotional involvement in the leader's goals, identification with the leader, follower and leader beliefs are similar, expression of warmth towards the leader, and follower confidence in goal achievement. In stressful situations followers look to their leaders to deliver them from their difficulties, so, the charismatic effects are more likely to occur when followers feel distress. Charismatic leadership works because it links followers and their self-concepts to the organizational identity.

Avolio, (1999) stated that transformational leadership is concerned with the performance of followers and with developing followers to their fullest potential. Those who exhibit transformational leadership are effective at motivating followers to act in ways that support the greater good instead of their own interests because they have a strong set of internal values and ideals. These leaders are deeply respected and imitated by followers. They provide followers with a clear vision and sense of mission.

Transformational leadership is clearly best utilized to create strategy and focus on organizational change. Leaders are less concerned with daily workflow and processes, so sometimes transformational leadership lacks attention to details. Leaders must sustain both a great deal of motivation and passion for long periods of time.

Burns (1978) describes transactional leadership as leaders who focus on the exchanges that happen between leaders and their followers. In contrast to transformational leadership, managers who offer promotions to employees who surpass their goals are transactional leaders. In the classroom, the teacher is transactional when the student receives a grade for the work that is completed. Transactional leaders do not individualize the needs of their followers nor do they focus on their personal development. Transactional leaders exchange things of value with followers to advance their own as well as their followers' agendas. These leaders are influential because it is in the best interest of the followers to do what the leader wants (Kuhnert & Lewis, 1987)

While transactional leadership results in expected outcomes, transformational leadership results in performance that goes beyond what is expected. Individuals who exhibited transformational leadership were perceived to be more proficient leaders with better performance outcomes than individuals who exhibited only transactional leadership (Lowe, et al., 1996). Transformational leadership produces greater outcomes than transactional leadership.

Transactional leadership is the best approach for maximizing operational efficiency. In the areas of innovation, long-term strategies and employee development, transactional leadership often falls short.

Neither transactional or transformational leadership is a question of good or bad. These forms of leadership are opposite approaches to leadership and are applied based upon certain types of situations. Both forms of leadership can be utilized and integrated into one blended approach. To adapt and apply these two styles of leadership, leaders must consider the advantages and disadvantages of each style as well as the current operations that their organization is functioning in.

When adjusted and applied with social learning theory, transformational and transactional leadership blended assists the organization grow and achieve its goals by utilizing internal and external assets more effectively. Leaders are able to adjust more proficiently to internal and external changes that affect the organization.

Bandura, A. (1977). *Social Learning Theory*. New York: General Learning Press.

Bandura, A. & Walters, R. (1963). *Social Learning and Personality Development*. New York: Holt, Rinehart & Winston.

Bryman, A. (1992). *Charisma and leadership in organizations*. London: Sage.

Burns, J.M. (1978). *Leadership*. New York: Harper & Row.

House, R.J. (1976). *A 1976 theory of charismatic leadership*. In J.G. Hunt & L.L. Larson (Eds.),*Leadership: The cutting edge* (pp. 189-207). Carbondale: Southern Illinois University Press.

Kuhnert, K.W. (1994). *Transforming leadership: Developing people through delegation*. In B. M. Bass & B.J. Avilio (Eds.), *Improving organizational effectiveness through transformational leadership* (pp. 10-25). Thousand Oaks, CA: Sage

Kuhnert, K.W. & Lewis, P. (1987). Transactional and transformational leadership: A constructive/developmental analysis. *Academy of Management Review*, 12(4), 648-657.

Lowe, K.B., Krock, K.G., & Sivasubramaniam, N. (1996). Effectiveness correlates of transformational and transactional leadership: A meta-analytic review of the MLQ literature. *Leadership Quarterly*, 7(3), 385-425.

Miller, N. & Dollard, J. (1941). *Social Learning and Imitation*. New Haven, NJ: Yale University Press.

Statistics of Peer Pressure

Researchers have established that there are numerous pressures that are experienced by teens aged 12-17. B. Larsen, et.al suggests that these pressures include: academic achievement (61%); personal appearance (29% felt that they had to look good); be a part of a social peer group (28%); involve themselves in extracurricular activities (especially athletics) (21%); and experience drug and alcohol (4 % and 6%). Based on this information, peer pressure is much more than someone asking you to experiment with alcohol or drugs.

Gender can affect how these pressures are internalized and expressed. Of the teens who were surveyed, 29% responded that they felt pressure to look good. Girls were more likely than boys to state that they felt pressure to look good (35% to 23%).

Peer Pressure Explained

Peer pressure affects people of all ages and transcends all age groups. Whether positive or negative, peer pressure is any type of influence that comes as a result of interaction within a peer group. Although this peer group may be age related (within an age range), the group may be identified by commonalities such as motherhood, professional affiliations or local neighborhoods. Since peer pressure can happen throughout one's life; teens, young adults and adults must learn to develop self-confidence and surround themselves with positive influences.

While their identities are still forming, young people are more susceptible to peer pressure. Young people desire to fit into their peer groups and do not want to be bullied. A combination of age-related and developmental factors contributes to youth increasingly feeling open to peer pressure. Some of those factors include: punishment, loss, risk taking, more vulnerable to the effects of reward and the quest for immediate versus delayed gratification.

Societal expectations and peer judgment or influence affects adults. Many adults face the pressures of academic achievement and career advancement. There is great pressure to maintain an image in the work, social and/or neighborhood environments.

Peer pressure can be experienced from people without them saying anything to you (implicit peer pressure). Pressure can also be experienced from direct remarks made by members of a group (explicit peer pressure).

Subtle pressure or implicit peer pressure happens when one is pulled into conforming to a social group to increase the chances of being accepted. Situations, such as seeing others who are considered cool drinking or smoking illegal substances at a party.

Explicit peer pressure is much easier to detect and recognize. Others in the group say don't worry, let's just have some fun. One becomes a part of the group by participating in an activity that they are not comfortable with. Sometimes there is the threat that you will not be a member of the group if you don't actively participate.

Risks

Serious and life-altering consequences are associated with the risks related to peer pressure. These consequences are not usually immediately obvious or they may not seem real. Some of these risks are associated with substance abuse and sexual situations.

Use of substances such as alcohol and cannabis can lead to problems with substance abuse. Youth can adversely affect their brain development and negatively affect their adult health. Issues such as heart disease, high blood pressure and sleep disorders can be by-products of substance abuse.

Peer pressure can lead to a person engaging in sexual activity before they are prepared for the consequences. Some consequences may include exposure to sexually transmitted infection (STI), developing pregnancy, or having images of your activities posted online without your knowledge or consent.

Whether online or in person, being pressured by peers can lead to stressful experiences. Excessive worry may be developed as a result of your loss of sense of identity and/or self-confidence.

Peer Influence

Positive peer pressure or peer influence can occur anytime one peer is more influential than the other. Peer pressure is not always negative. There are instances where individuals attempt to fit into a healthy social group of peers getting good grades, joining sports teams, joining positive associations or groups making plans for their futures. When seeing someone else performing positive and challenging activities, peer influence can show that there is support, encouragement and community available. Peer influence offers one the opportunity to make intelligent life choices, develop healthy goals and identify where it is best for you to concentrate your time and talents.

Rising Above Peer Pressure

Not giving into the influence of others to act in a certain way, means that you can rise above peer pressure. Regardless of your age, socioeconomic background or other identifiers, you can practice not relenting to negative peer pressure and focus on surrounding yourself with positive influences. Resisting negative peer pressure may involve avoiding those who attempt to pressure you, saying no, or surrounding yourself with positive people.

Parents can positively affect/influence their children. Most children do not want to disappoint their parents. Honest and open communication with the adolescent son or daughter that explains the positive and negative influences that can affect their lives even into adulthood will provide the adolescent with valuable information that can affect their decision making. By being understanding, parents positively influence their children's behaviors.

Bibliography

1.Larsen, Brett, et.al. American Psychological Association. Speaking of psychology: the good and bad of peer pressure.

2.Barbalat, G., et.al. [risk-taking in adolescence: a neuroeconomics approach]. 2010:36(2):147-54.

3.Centers for Disease Control and Prevention. Teen substance use and risk.

4.Widman, L., et.al. Adolescent susceptibility to peer influence in sexual situations.2016;58(3):323-329.

LEAP PERSPECTIVE

FIRST PERSPECTIVE: CRITERION 1&2

ROAD TO SUCCESS

Every day you may need one or more of the different Leap words from each category to get back on track to succeed during the day. Once you get the right combination of words to get you through the day, from each category, take at least three (3) minutes to meditate on each word and its meaning in your life.

More importantly, take 10 minutes to use the words to write a poem to a loved one or someone who has had a positive influence in your life (e.g., parent, friend, teacher, etc.).

RARE-9 PERSPECTIVE OR CLIMBING THE LADDER

SECOND PERSPECTIVE: CRITERION 1, 3&4

When you have reached the endless road and feel deflated, use the RARE perspective to get back on track.

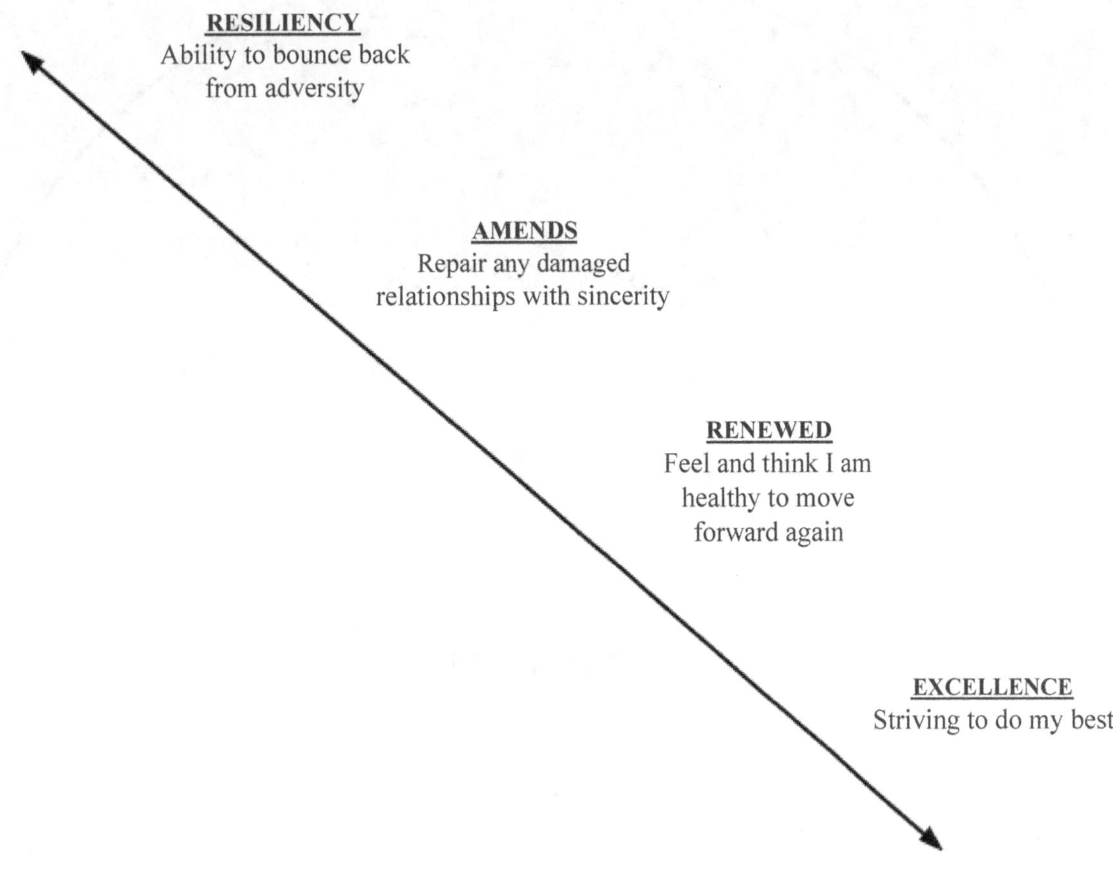

Using the scale above, circle the number you feel will reflect how well you can conclude the remainder of the day from "Good" to "Very Good".

CONVERSATION PERSPECTIVE

THIRD PERSPECTIVE: ALL CRITERION

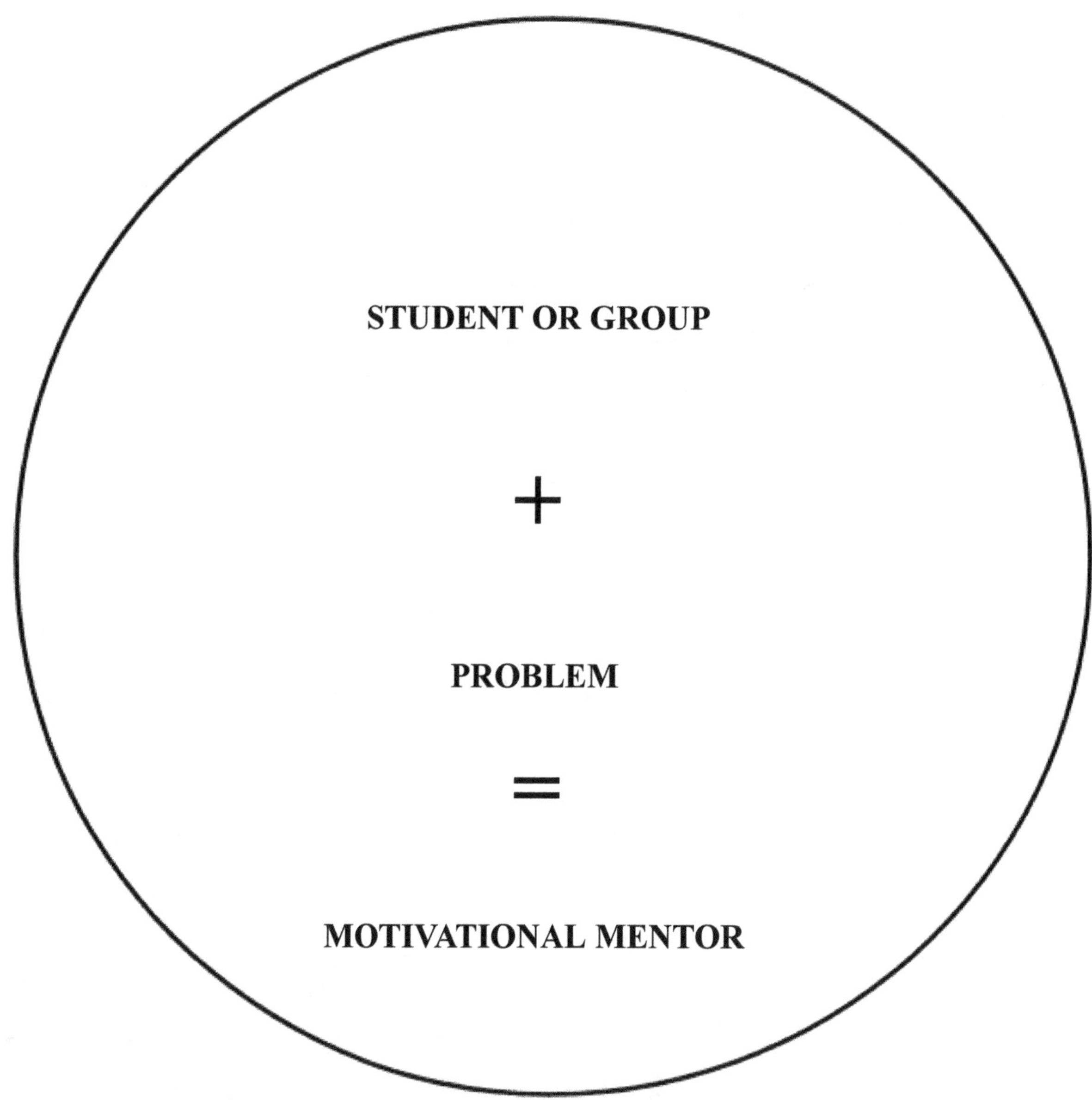

The objective is the resolution, due to an existing problem.

What was accomplished during the conversation? (Note: no one ever fails)

IMMEDIATE CONFLICT RESOLUTION & TANGO:

FACE-TO-FACE VIRTUAL PROCESS

The virtual face-to-face conversation is available when a mentee **needs** an immediate resolution or mentor connection. The Tango process is initiated by parents, guardians, mentees, mentors, or possible school officials in support of the mentee. However, the mentees have a process that he has to work through with his mentor. The virtual process saves time, quicker line of communication with mentor, and an ability to see emotions happening with the mentee and enables mentors to redirect mentee based on facial expressions.

TANGO PROGRAM:

EACH OF THE FIVE (5) COMPONENTS WILL REQUIRE OF FIVE (5) MINUTES MAXIMUM TIME TO DISCUSS THE ISSUE FROM EITHER MENTOR/ MENTEE, PARENTS/GUARDIANS AND POSSIBLY SCHOOL ADMINISTRATORS.

1. Share problem(s)/concerns.

2. Mediation time.

3. Mentor reflection/Feedback.

4. Mentor and mentee's resolution/outcome.

5. Mentor reports back to RARE-9 Jaguar Mentorship Program **within** twenty-hours with details and finalization of the Tango process.

RARE-9 JAGUAR MENTORSHIP ORGANIZATION

"THREE IMPORTANT LEADERSHIP STYLES"
(Mentee/Mentees please define the following words below.)

1.   SELF-LEADERSHIP.

2.   TRANSFORMATIONAL LEADERSHIP.

3.   TRANSACTIONAL LEADERSHIP.

I Will Not Die an Unlived Life

(Dawna Markova)

I will not die an unlived life.
I will not live in fear
Of falling or catching fire.
I choose to inhabit my days,
To allow my living to open me,
To make me less afraid,
More accessible,
To loosen my heart
Until it becomes a wing,
A torch, a promise.
I choose to risk my significance,
To live so that which came to me as seed
Goes to the next as blossom
And that which came to me as blossom,
Goes on as fruit.

*** Their Name Is Today ***

*** Reclaiming Childhood in a Hostile World ***

By Johann Christoph Arnold

FOREWORD BY MARK K. SHRIVER

Johann Christoph Arnold

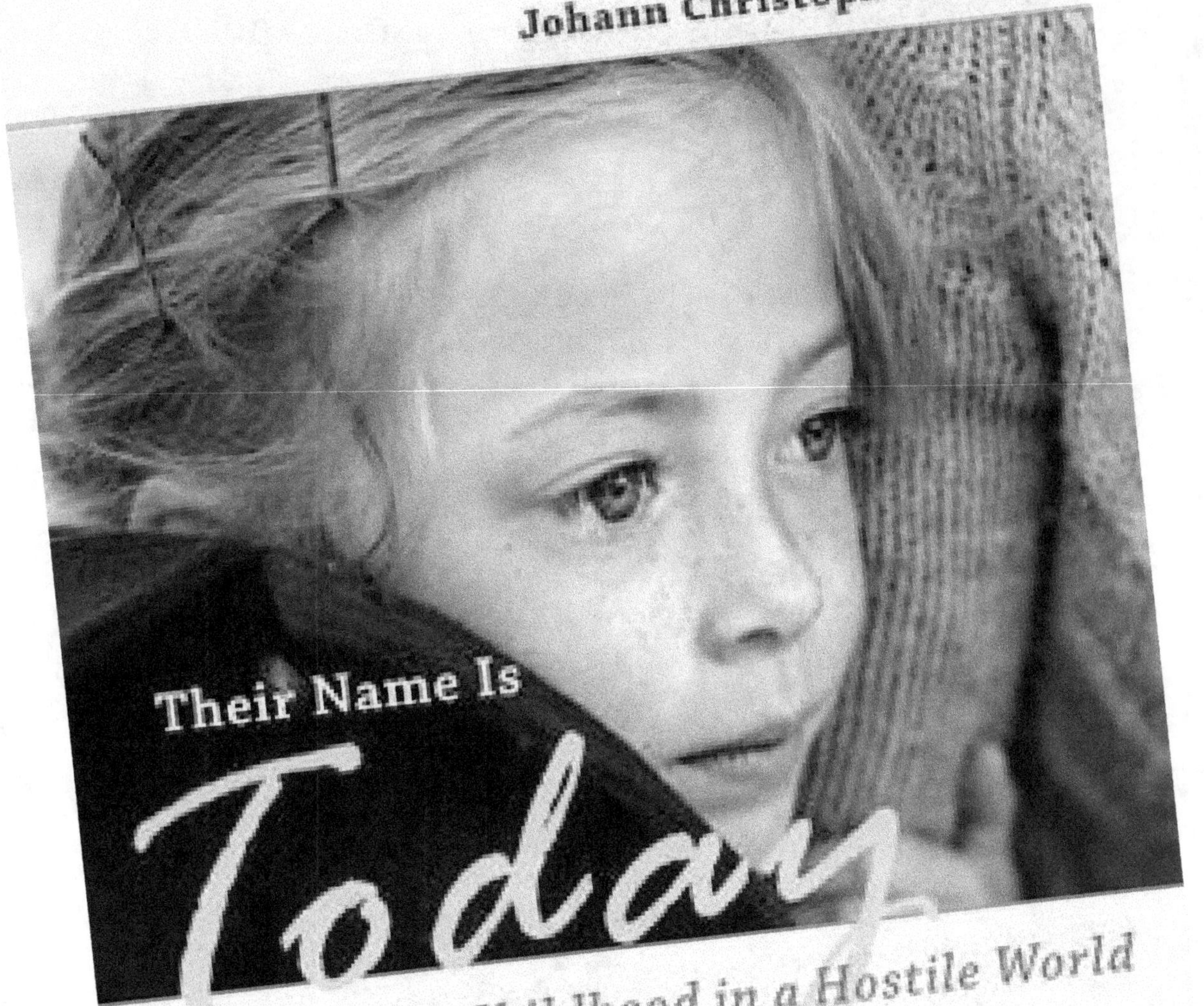

FOREWORD BY MARK K. SHRIVER

Study Confirms School-to-Prison Pipeline

New **research** found that early strict discipline causes an increase in adult crime.

By <u>Lauren Camera</u>

July 27, 2021

Save **(D@@Q**

Students assigned to stricter middle schools are 3.2 percentage points more likely to have been arrested, 2.5

percentage points more likely to have been **incarcerated** as adults. They were also 1.7 **percentage** points more likely to drop out of high school and 2.4

percentage points less likely to attend a four-year college. @

(SKYNESHER/GETTY IMAGES)

Children who attend schools with high suspension rates are significantly more likely to be arrested and jailed as adults - especially Black and Hispanic boys - according to new research that shines a spotlight on the school-to-prison pipeline.

Data have long shown that Black and Hispanic students experience suspension and expulsion at much higher rates than white students, and that as adults, they're also disproportionately represented in the county's prison system. And while research shows a correlation between high levels of education and low levels of criminal activity, there exists little evidence on the role that individual schools can play in their students' future.

Researchers from Boston University, the University of Colorado Boulder and Harvard University sought to find whether a causal link exists between students who experience strict school discipline and being arrested or incarcerated as an adult, and whether attending a stricter school influences criminal activity in adulthood.

"Our findings show that early censure of school misbehavior causes increases in adult crime - that there is, in fact, a school-to-prison pipeline," the researchers wrote in an article published Tuesday in Education Next. "Any effort to maintain safe and orderly school climates must take into account the clear and negative consequences of exclusionary discipline practices for young students, and especially young students of color, which last well into adulthood."

Specifically, students assigned to stricter middle schools are 3.2 percentage points more likely to have been arrested, 2.5 percentage points more likely to have been incarcerated as adults. They were also 1.7 percentage points more likely to drop out of high school and 2.4 percentage points less likely to attend a four-year college.

DeVos argued that the guidance did a disservice to schools, creating disruptive classrooms where teachers felt unsafe because they were pressured by school administrators to report students' safety, the decision to revoke the guidance followed a report of recommendations from the White House school safety commission, formed in the wake of a 2018 school shooting in Parkland, Florida.

At the time, Democrats ripped DeVos for flouting long-standing civil rights concerns about the alarming rate at which Black and Hispanic boys and girls are disciplined compared to white students, a phenomenon that begins as early as kindergarten.

Now, the Education Department's Office for Civil Rights under the Biden administration is poised to reinstate much of the Obama-era guidance, including putting schools on ntice for disproportionate rates and severity of school discipline, school discipline data collection, an emphasis on social and emotional learning and support and training for teachers and other school staff.

"Misbehaving peers can have strong negative impacts on other students in the classroom, and all students need a safe, predictable, and peaceful environment to thrive," the research concludes. "But our findings show that the school-to-prison pipeline is real and poses substantial risks for students in strict school environments."

What's less clear, however, is where the Biden administration stands on the use of police officers or school resource officers in schools, and whether the Education Department is prepared to weigh in on the topic in any significant way.

Despite the racial reckoning that took hold in communities across the country in the wake of the death of George Floyd - one that included efforts to sever school district contracts with local police departments - Cardona has been outspoken in his early tenure about the positive aspects of having a dedicated law enforcement officer inside schools based on his experience in Connecticut.

The new findings released Tuesday did not address the issue of school resource officers, but the researchers argue that their findings pose a critical question for policymakers, educators and school leaders.

"For whom are our schools safe?" they ask. "As the nation continues to grapple with questions about racial equity and police reform, the contributing causal role that school discipline practices play in raising the risk of criminality in adulthood can't be ignored."

The impacts are significantly more predictive for Black and Hispanic boys who attended strict middle schools.

Editorial Cartoons on Education

The researchers also found that **principals,** who often oversee the suspension and expulsion of students, were the "major driver" in the frequency and severity of school discipline, and in tracking the movement of principals from one school to another, they found that a principal who doled out **high** numbers or **suspensions** and expulsions in **one** school would do the same at **the** next.

The findings come as Education Secretary Miguel Cardona and department officials seek public comments on new regulations related to school discipline and the disproportionate rate at which students of color are suspended and expelled.

Under former Education Secretary Betsy DeVos, the department **rescinded** a slate of Obama-era civil rights regulations **aimed** at preventing schools from disproportionately disciplining Black and Hispanic **students** and students with disabilities.

RARE-9 Mentee Progress Report

EXAMPLE

Name _________________________   Date:__________

RARE-9 JAGUAR
MENTORSHIP ORGANIZATION

Progress Report

Goals

Progress

Feedback

EXAMPLE

:::::::::

Attendance Sheet

RARE-9 JAGUAR
MENTORSHIP ORGANIZATION

EVENT:	DATE:

No	Student Name	Time In	Time Out	Signature
1				
2				
3				
4				
5				
6				
7				
8				
9				
10				
11				
12				
13				
14				
15				
16				
17				
18				
19				
20				
21				

RARE-9 Jaguar Mentorship Organization
Graduation Certificate
EXAMPLE

"The Good, BAD, Ugly"

" THE GOOD "

WACH Columbia
Story by Shamar Winston · Yesterday 11:40 AM
Three free teen nights for Columbia's youth
Follow

Free Events for Teens Ages 13–16
GAMES!
SNACKS!
MUSIC!
And More!

BLACK LIVES MATTER
BLACK LIVES

COLOR IS NOT A CRIME

'My daughter couldn't find a Black doll with afro hair — now we sell them'
by Annette Kellow · 12h

14-YEAR-OLD BLACK BRAINIAC HEADED TO SOUTHERN UNIVERSITY ON A FULL-RIDE SCHOLARSHIP
Atiya Jordan · March 11, 2022 · 15958

Elijah Precciely, at lectern, talks about how excited he is of becoming a Southern University student at the Board of Supervisors meeting. Image Credit: ADVOCATE STAFF PHOTO BY BILL FEIG

Talk to Young Kids About Racism and Racial Bias
Black Teen Activists Are Making All of Our Futures Better

NBC News
Follow

Rash of violence has not deterred Black parents from keeping their kids at HBCUs
Story by Curtis Bunn · 1d

Kim and Tommy Sturdivant said they didn't consider pulling their two children — son Seth at Morgan State University and daughter Mia at Howard University — out of school after the rash of gun violence that struck historically Black colleges and universities across the country earlier this month.

CBS News

Carolina Panorama Newspaper · August 9 - 15, 2023

Community leaders urged to help eradicate illiteracy

Calling 100 Black Pastors, Mentors, Ministry Leaders, Brotherhood, Men's Organizations, Business Owners, Barbers, Stylists and Concerned Parents. It's kickoff season! School is back in and the punts are being punted. The time has come for kids to get down to the business of education, being educated. This year we are going for the goal, eradicating illiteracy and raising the academic scores in SC and around the nation.

On Saturday, August 19, 2023 at 8:00 AM at Embassy Suites Hotel 200 Stoneridge Drive in Columbia, SC, meet some 100 Black authors as they discuss winning strategies via vision boards for our kids this academic season.

According to reports from the SC Department of Education, in 2021 out of 15,652 Black or African-American stu-

Black teenagers should learn about money before they graduate high school

Story by insider@insider.com (Sarah Enelow-Snyder) · 7h

Find a Qualified Financial Advisor

Boy who walked 6 miles to middle school graduation gets college scholarship

Xavier Jones spent two ho[urs] [walkin]g to his middle school graduation. It inspired a university president to give him a college sc[holarship.] [Steve] Hartman has the story in "On the Road."

Sidney Keys III, 16

Kevin Mazur/Getty Images for CNN
© Provided by Parents

Literacy Advocate, Atlanta, Georgia

Growing up in St. Louis, Sidney Keys III loved to lose himself in books. What he didn't like was that many of the books he enjoyed reading didn't have stories, or faces on the covers, like his. Perhaps it was because statistics show that boys don't score well in literacy. Keys set out on a mission to make reading fun for his peers. At 10 years old, he started Books N Bros, the first and only youth-led monthly book club for Gen Z Black boys that now has members throughout the U.S., Canada, and Europe. The club's motto is, "Cool Bros Read." By the time he turned 11, Sidney had been featured on CNN.

Inside Edition

10-Year-Old Allegedly Steals

SUV to Drive to His Mother

Meet David, A 9-Yr-Old Mensa Member Who Just Graduated From High School

Story by Beverly L Jenkins · 12h ago

Parenting often means meeting your children where where they are. Instead of forcing a square peg into a round hole, it's our job to nurture their interests and encourage them to think outside the box, even when it comes to traditional education. Or, if your child happens to be "profoundly gifted" like Ronya Balogun's son, David, you have to be willing to smash the box to bits and forge a new path forward!

"The BAD"

Atlanta school under federal investigation after allegations principal assigned Black students to classes based on race

FS Raw Story

Cops still on force despite calling Black kids 'ghetto' and 'a pack of animals': rep...

Story by Sky Palma • Yesterday 12:48 PM

383

👍 Like   💬 159 Comments

The Department of Education's Office for Civil Rights has launched an investigation into an Atlanta public elementary school after allegation: ... principal was assigning Black students to certain classes.

In the letter provided to CNN, the Office for Civil Rights said it will investigate allegations of discrimination based on race and whether Atlanta Public Schools ...bjected students at the school to different treatment based on race." It will also look into whether the district retaliated against the complainant.

YOUR CHILDREN ARE YOU BUT

DOES IT MAKE YOU ANGRY TO SEE YOURSELF

Racial trauma and generational trauma are in... ...ined because racial ... be passed down generationally. For example, when Black families have "the talk" with their kids about racism and ...iety and how to handle situations with police, that is based on experiences of being discriminated against and traumatized because of skin color.

That itself is a form of generational-racial trauma because you have to explain this to your kid, and it's not because you want to, it's because society still disavows, dehumanizes, discriminates, and ostracizes Black people and people of color just because of their skin.

Most clinicians are not trained to pay attention to racial trauma and are unable to actually assess it, or notice the symptoms and signs of it. But if you find a therapist that specializes in this form of trauma, going to therapy can be very helpful in noticing how this trauma manifests itself physically, mentally, emotionally, relationally, and spiritually in your body.

We don't want to talk about race, and particularly whiteness, in our society

Teen Vogue

Corporal Punishment in Schools: Black Students Suffer Physical Abuse in the Classroom

Story by Kameisha Smith • 8h ago

On the heels of hate flyers placed on the marquees of three Black churches in Columbia, elected leaders gathered at Mt. Calvary Missionary Baptist Church, showing solidarity i...

FS New York Post

Private school sicced FBI on us when we protested critical race theory, moms claim

Study Confirms School-to-Prison Pipeline

New research found that early strict discipline causes an increase in adult crime.

By Lauren Camera

Florida's Racial Outrage: Black Students Traumatized in Shocking Racially Segregated Assembly

©Provided by Mama Say What?!

Flagler County, Florida, has found itself at the epicenter of an unfolding education controversy. Black students at Bunnell Elementary School were unexpectedly pulled out from their classes to attend an assembly about their underwhelming performance on standardized tests. Here's the full story.

"The Ugly"

Teen killed after shoplifting allegations remembered as 'intelligent, humorous'

Under former Education Secretary Betsy DeVos, the department rescinded a slate of Obama-era civil rights regulations aimed at preventing schools from disproportionately disciplining Black and Hispanic students and students with disabilities.

Children who attend schools with high suspension rates are significantly more likely to be arrested and jailed as adults – especially Black and Hispanic boys – according to new research that shines a spotlight on the school-to-prison pipeline.

"Our findings show that early censure of school misbehavior causes increases in adult crime – that there is, in fact, a school-to-prison pipeline," the researchers wrote in an

View Profile

+ Follow

WACH Columbia

Florida's Racial Outrage: Black Students Traumatized in Shocking Racially Segregated Assembly

Story by J. Lysikatos • 9h

9-year-old shot and killed in Richland County identified by coroner

Columbia WIS TV

Convicted killer Jeroid Price returns to custody in South Carolina

Story by Tiffany Tran-Ozuna • 3h ago

---Thy Black Man

African Americans: PARENTS – Violence As Discipline Must Stop.

Story by Staff - Jan 25

(**ThyBlackMan.com**) For far too long *African Americans* have acted just like the definition of "black" in the dictionary – dismal, gloomy, devoid of moral character, evil etc. This is especially true when it comes to how our people have disciplined our children – with spankings that are far too close to outright child abuse.

Today such "discipline" is dangerous and largely unproductive for many reasons. First it's illegal and you could end up in jail. And you as a "black" person do not want to get caught up in the system of bond/bail, hearings, jail time, community service, DHS/DFACS etc. Secondly, children should be respected as well because they have civil, constitutional and God-given rights – whether you agree and like those rights or not. If your parent(s) ignored those rights, they were wrong too but don't keep the cycle of ignorance and mistakes going.

BIN: Black Information Network

Black Student Banned From Prom, Graduation After Being Shot 10 Times

Story by Jovonne Ledet • Yesterday 11:41 AM

RARE-9 JAGUAR MENTORSHIP ORGANIZATION ADMISSION PACKAGE

EXAMPLE

RARE-9 JAGUAR MENTORSHIP ORGANIZATION

406 Flume Road Elgin, South Carolina 29045

Rare9jaguar.com

EXAMPLE

Parent/Guardian Consent Form

Date: _______________________________

Your permission is requested for your sons, _______________________________________ to

participate in our RARE-9 Jaguar Mentorship Program.

Mentoring is based on a trusting, respectful, empathy, and role model type behavior between the mentor and mentee. The mentor will keep mentee information confidential and boundaries in place at all times.

You will be notified under the following circumstances:

1. The mentee reveals information about hurting himself or someone else.
2. The mentee is in physical danger.

By signing this form, I give my informed consent for my child to participate in the RARE-9 Jaguar Mentorship Program. I understand that anything that my child shares will be kept confidential except in the above-mentioned situations.

Parent/Guardian____ Date_______________

This consent will be on file throughout the time your child attends our program. You may revoke this consent at any time. Please feel free to call this organization if you have any questions or concerns at ###-###- ####. We will be happy to talk with you.

PLEASE COMPLETE THIS FORM AND SEND IT BACK WITH YOUR SON ASAP.

RARE-9 JAGUAR MENTORSHIP ACTIVITIES

Parental Consent Form
EXAMPLE

Name____ Age_______ Birth Date__________

Address____

City____ State___________________ Zip code _______________

Student Email____ Mobile Phone ___________________________

Emergency Contact Details:

Name ____ Relation to Student: __________________

Home Phone Number ____________________ Mobile / Work Phone Number ___________________

Parent Email address: ___________________________

Medical Information:

Name of Doctor________________________________ Doctor's Phone Number___________________

Does your child suffer from any condition requiring medical treatment including medication?
If yes, please specify____
____
____
____

- **I give permission** for my child to take part in the activities provided by the Rare 9 Jaguar Mentorship program and for the information to be held and used by the Rare- 9 Jaguar Mentorship team
- **I give permission** for Acts Trust to use photo and video footage taken during the activities for promotional purposes such as displays and video presentations of our work.
- **I give permission** for medical attention 10 be sought in case of emergency.
- **I understand** that the Rare 9 Jaguar Mentorship Team cannot take responsibility if your child does not abide by the Rules.
- **I permit** my Child's email and mobile number to be given to The Rare 9 Jaguar Mentorship team to be used for emergency and event promotional use.

Dated _________________________ Signature____

Relationship _________________ Full Name____

Please complete and send with your child to the activities

For further information call ###-###-#### or email ********@***.COM

EXAMPLE

CONSENT FORM FOR PHOTOS/PICTURES TAKEN

Date:_________________________________

The RARE-9 Jaguar Mentorship Organization is requesting your permission for your son to take photos/pictures while in the RARE-9 Jaguar Mentorship Program. The photos/pictures will only be used to support this organization. The photos/pictures will not be sold or distributed to any other business or organization.

Parent/Guardian Signature

____

Name of Mentee:

____

Date:____

Cost of Mentee Attendance into Program

EXAMPLE

Date:_______________________________

NAME OF MENTEE:____

WHAT SERVICES ARE BEING PROVIDED;_____________________________

AMOUNT DUE: $____________

DUE DATE OF PAYMENT: ____________________

PAYMENT RECEIVED BY: <u>Minister RARE-9</u>

TITLE/POSITION: <u>RARE-9 CO-CEO</u>

*******PLEASE NOTE WHICH PAYMENT TYPES YOU ACCEPT HERE EX. CHECKS AND CASH ONLY ETC. *********

RARE-9 JAGUAR MENTORSHIP ORGANIZATION
406 Flume Road Elgin, South Carolina 29045
Rare9jaguar.com

COST OF PROGRAM
EXAMPLE

1. Initial Mentor Intake: $70.00

2. Weekly Mentee meetings are: $75.00

3. Monthly Mentee meetings are: $300.00

4. Only want Immediate Conflict Resolution & Tango: Face-To-Face Virtual Process. Weekly $75.00/ Monthly $300.

5. It is free when parents/guardians call the mentor for assistance with a crisis, concern, or issue concerning the mentee.

*****Please note that any other charges for program services can be discussed/negotiated.****

Business Plan

RARE-9 Jaguar Mentorship Organization
406 Flume Rd. Elgin, SC 29045, USA

January 14,2024

EXAMPLE

Executive Summary

The Company

(Here write a Brief explanation about the backstory to your business. How did it come to be.)

The Ownership

(Here you would specify how the company will be structured as. ie Nonprofit.)

The Management

(Here you would indicate the name of the person who will manage the company.)

Business Plan - RARE-9 Jaguar Mentorship Organization

The Goals and Objectives

RARE -9 JAGUAR MENTORSHIP ORGANIZATION

MISSION

(Here explain your company mission)

(Special Mission)

(Here define the special mission of your business.)

Business Plan - RARE-9 Jaguar Mentorship Organization

The Services

(Here you are also outlining what services your company will be providing. You can reference to your Vision page of the business plan if the information is listed there.)

The Target Market

(Here you would describe who your ideal client is by outlining the following information.)
The Company's target market has the following Characteristics:

- *Age:*

- *Gender:*

- *Marital status:*

Pricing Strategy

(Here you would explain your pricing strategy that's being used in your business.)

Capital Requirements

(Here you would list and Identify your business start-up costs and list them.)

The Company

Business Sector

(Here you would Identify the specific area or classification that your business would

 be considered to be under.)

Company Background

(Here you would again explain the background story of your business and what were

some if not all the determining reasons for you putting it together.)

RARE-9 JAGUAR MENTORSHIP ORGANIZATION

MISSION

(Here outline your company/organization mission.)

(Special Mission)

(Here outline more information pertaining to your company/organization mission.)

Business Plan - RARE-9 Jaguar Mentorship Organization

Company Ownership Structure

(Here state how your business/organization will be structured as. (ie. Non profit)

Ownership Background

(Here you would include your credentials that help to establish your credibility as a business owner in this niche. Include the owner's name and all training, certifications and licenses.)

- *Owner: Owners name goes here*
- *Experiences and training: Here you would list Your experiences and Training.*

You can make reference to other documents that are within your business plan that contains this information.

Company Management Structure

(Here note by whom the company will be managed by. This is also a good place to list the Board of Directors.)

Company Assets

(Here list your company assets. If your home is being used for business purposes. That can be noted here also. Vehicles and their value can also be listed

Business Plan - RARE-9 Jaguar Mentorship Organization

Services

The Services

(Here you outline the services that your organization will provide. You can also refer to other documentation that may be located in other parts of your Business plan such as the Vision.)

Proprietary Rights

(Here you would indicate what license(s) you would hold to operate your business.)

Future Services

(Here you would identify the next steps for the future of your business and who it will help.)

Business Plan - RARE-9 Jaguar Mentorship Organization

Marketing Plan

The Target Market

(Here you would list the characteristics of your customer. Who will you be serving

in your organization?)

- *Their age*
- *Their Gender*
- *Their MArital Status*

Location Analysis

(Here you would indicate what city and state your business will operate in. In addition,

you can list services that are nearby that your business can help and benefit from.)

Pricing

(Here you can list the type of strategy your company will use as a payment method.)

Business Plan - RARE-9 Jaguar Mentorship Organization

Advertising

(Here you would list the methods that your business will be promoted through.)

- online channels(website, google ads etc

- Social Media

- Tv or radio: ads

- Print (magazines, flyers, etc).

SWOT Analysis

Strengths

(Here you would write out a statement detailing the specific strengths of your business.)

Weaknesses

(Here you can write out what possible challenges your company has faced and how you either overcame them or identify the steps you are taking to overcome them.)

Business Plan - RARE-9 Jaguar Mentorship Organization

Opportunities

(Here you can specify the benefits that your business will bring to the community, city, state and world as a whole.)

Threats

(Here you would list anything you believe that would be considered as a threat to your business. If you deem there to be no threats, you would specify that also.)

Daily Operations

(Here you would list details pertaining to the daily operational flow of your business. Include who your business will be helping and in what ways you will be helping them. You can also specify the hours of operation daily.)

Operations Facilities

(Here you would provide the details about the building your business is located in or at. If you currently don't have your own building you can specify that here along

with your future goals to obtain one.)

Staffing

(Here you would specify the details on the formation of your organizational chart. If this information is located within another section of your business plan, you can indicate a reference to that section.)

Suppliers

(Here you would list the sources that would be used to provide you with materials needed to run your business This could include people, persons and things in the form of organizations and schools.)

Business Plan - RARE-9 Jaguar Mentorship Organization

<u>Financials</u>

Capital Requirements

(Here you would list any investments that have been already made toward the business along with the value of those items. Also include any additional money that would be needed. This information can be formatted in the form of a projected income statement. Be sure to include the projected costs for Marketing, Insurance, Rent, Utilities, Licenses, Salaries and Benefits, and any interest. After itemizing your projected income statement, provide the total dollar amount of all expenses listed.)

Remember

This business plan serves as an

EXAMPLE

for informational purposes only.